If Lost, Please Return To:

_____

Monday

Today's Goals

Tuesday

Today's Goals

Wednesday

Today's Goals

Thursday

Today's Goals

Friday

Today's Goals

Saturday

Today's Goals

Sunday

Today's Goals

Notes

Bible Study

Date:

Today's Study

Scripture

_____

_____

_____

_____

_____

_____

_____

_____

_____

_____

_____

_____

_____

_____

_____

_____

_____

_____

_____

_____

_____

_____

Praise

Prayer

S.O.A.P.

Scripture

Observation

Application

Prayer

Reflection

What Is This Scripture Telling Me?

_____

_____

_____

_____

Why Did God Include This Scripture In The Bible?

_____

_____

_____

_____

What Do I Need To Further Study From This Verse?

_____

_____

_____

_____

Bible Study   Date:

Today's Study

Scripture

Praise

Prayer

S.O.A.P.

Scripture

Observation

Application

Prayer

Reflection

What Is This Scripture Telling Me?

_____

_____

_____

_____

Why Did God Include This Scripture In The Bible?

_____

_____

_____

_____

What Do I Need To Further Study From This Verse?

_____

_____

_____

_____

Bible Study Date:

Today's Study

Scripture

_____

_____

_____

_____

_____

_____

_____

_____

_____

_____

_____

_____

_____

_____

_____

_____

_____

Praise

Prayer

S.O.A.P.

Scripture

Observation

Application

Prayer

Reflection

What Is This Scripture Telling Me?

_____

_____

_____

_____

Why Did God Include This Scripture In The Bible?

_____

_____

_____

_____

What Do I Need To Further Study From This Verse?

_____

_____

_____

_____

Bible Study

Date:

Today's Study

Scripture

_____

_____

_____

_____

_____

_____

_____

_____

_____

_____

_____

_____

_____

_____

_____

_____

Praise

Prayer

S.O.A.P.

Scripture

Observation

Application

Prayer

Reflection

What Is This Scripture Telling Me?

_____

_____

_____

_____

Why Did God Include This Scripture In The Bible?

_____

_____

_____

_____

What Do I Need To Further Study From This Verse?

_____

_____

_____

_____

Bible Study

Date:

Today's Study

Scripture

_____

_____

_____

_____

_____

_____

_____

_____

_____

_____

_____

_____

_____

_____

_____

_____

_____

_____

_____

_____

Praise

Prayer

S.O.A.P.

Scripture	Observation

Application	Prayer

Reflection

What Is This Scripture Telling Me?

Why Did God Include This Scripture In The Bible?

What Do I Need To Further Study From This Verse?

Bible Study
Date:

Today's Study

Scripture

Praise

Prayer

S.O.A.P.

Scripture

Observation

Application

Prayer

Reflection

What Is This Scripture Telling Me?

_____

_____

_____

_____

Why Did God Include This Scripture In The Bible?

_____

_____

_____

_____

What Do I Need To Further Study From This Verse?

_____

_____

_____

_____

Bible Study Date:

Today's Study

Scripture

Praise

Prayer

S.O.A.P.

Scripture	Observation

Application	Prayer

Reflection

What Is This Scripture Telling Me?

_____

_____

_____

_____

Why Did God Include This Scripture In The Bible?

_____

_____

_____

_____

What Do I Need To Further Study From This Verse?

_____

_____

_____

_____

Monday

Today's Goals

Tuesday

Today's Goals

Wednesday

Today's Goals

Thursday

Today's Goals

Friday

Today's Goals

Saturday

Today's Goals

Sunday

Today's Goals

Notes

Bible Study   Date:

Today's Study

Scripture

Praise

Prayer

S.O.A.P.

Scripture

Observation

Application

Prayer

Reflection

What Is This Scripture Telling Me?

_____

_____

_____

_____

Why Did God Include This Scripture In The Bible?

_____

_____

_____

_____

What Do I Need To Further Study From This Verse?

_____

_____

_____

_____

Bible Study Date:

Today's Study

Scripture

Praise

Prayer

S.O.A.P.

Scripture

Observation

Application

Prayer

Reflection

What Is This Scripture Telling Me?

_____

_____

_____

_____

Why Did God Include This Scripture In The Bible?

_____

_____

_____

_____

What Do I Need To Further Study From This Verse?

_____

_____

_____

_____

Bible Study Date:

Today's Study

Scripture

Praise

Prayer

S.O.A.P.

Scripture	Observation

Application	Prayer

Reflection

What Is This Scripture Telling Me?

_____

_____

_____

_____

Why Did God Include This Scripture In The Bible?

_____

_____

_____

_____

What Do I Need To Further Study From This Verse?

_____

_____

_____

_____

Bible Study

Date:

Today's Study

Scripture

Praise

Prayer

S.O.A.P.

Scripture

Observation

Application

Prayer

Reflection

What Is This Scripture Telling Me?

_____

_____

_____

_____

Why Did God Include This Scripture In The Bible?

_____

_____

_____

_____

What Do I Need To Further Study From This Verse?

_____

_____

_____

_____

Bible Study   Date:

Today's Study

Scripture

_____
_____
_____
_____
_____
_____
_____
_____

_____
_____
_____
_____
_____
_____
_____
_____

Praise

Prayer

S.O.A.P.

Scripture

Observation

Application

Prayer

Reflection

What Is This Scripture Telling Me?

_____

_____

_____

_____

Why Did God Include This Scripture In The Bible?

_____

_____

_____

_____

What Do I Need To Further Study From This Verse?

_____

_____

_____

_____

Bible Study Date:

Today's Study

Scripture

Praise

Prayer

S.O.A.P.

Scripture

Observation

Application

Prayer

Reflection

What Is This Scripture Telling Me?

Why Did God Include This Scripture In The Bible?

What Do I Need To Further Study From This Verse?

Bible Study Date:

Today's Study

Scripture

Praise

Prayer

S.O.A.P.

Scripture

Observation

Application

Prayer

Reflection

What Is This Scripture Telling Me?

_____

_____

_____

_____

Why Did God Include This Scripture In The Bible?

_____

_____

_____

_____

What Do I Need To Further Study From This Verse?

_____

_____

_____

_____

Monday

Today's Goals

Tuesday

Today's Goals

Wednesday

Today's Goals

Thursday

Today's Goals

Friday

Today's Goals

Saturday

Today's Goals

Sunday

Today's Goals

Notes

Bible Study Date:

Today's Study

Scripture

Praise

Prayer

S.O.A.P.

Scripture

Observation

Application

Prayer

Reflection

What Is This Scripture Telling Me?

_____

_____

_____

_____

Why Did God Include This Scripture In The Bible?

_____

_____

_____

_____

What Do I Need To Further Study From This Verse?

_____

_____

_____

_____

Bible Study Date:

Today's Study

Scripture

Praise

Prayer

S.O.A.P.

Scripture

Observation

Application

Prayer

Reflection

What Is This Scripture Telling Me?

_____

_____

_____

_____

Why Did God Include This Scripture In The Bible?

_____

_____

_____

_____

What Do I Need To Further Study From This Verse?

_____

_____

_____

_____

Bible Study Date:

Today's Study

Scripture

_____
_____
_____
_____
_____
_____
_____
_____
_____
_____
_____
_____
_____
_____
_____
_____
_____
_____
_____
_____
_____

Praise

Prayer

S.O.A.P.

Scripture

Observation

Application

Prayer

Reflection

What Is This Scripture Telling Me?

_____

_____

_____

_____

Why Did God Include This Scripture In The Bible?

_____

_____

_____

_____

What Do I Need To Further Study From This Verse?

_____

_____

_____

_____

Bible Study Date:

Today's Study

Scripture

Praise

Prayer

S.O.A.P.

Scripture

Observation

Application

Prayer

Reflection

What Is This Scripture Telling Me?

_____

_____

_____

_____

Why Did God Include This Scripture In The Bible?

_____

_____

_____

_____

What Do I Need To Further Study From This Verse?

_____

_____

_____

_____

Bible Study Date:

Today's Study

Scripture

Praise

Prayer

S.O.A.P.

Scripture

Observation

Application

Prayer

Reflection

What Is This Scripture Telling Me?

_____
_____
_____
_____

Why Did God Include This Scripture In The Bible?

_____
_____
_____
_____

What Do I Need To Further Study From This Verse?

_____
_____
_____
_____

Bible Study Date:

Today's Study

Scripture

_____
_____
_____
_____
_____
_____
_____
_____
_____
_____
_____
_____
_____
_____
_____
_____
_____
_____
_____
_____
_____
_____
_____
_____

Praise

Prayer

S.O.A.P.

Scripture

Observation

Application

Prayer

Reflection

What Is This Scripture Telling Me?

_____

_____

_____

_____

Why Did God Include This Scripture In The Bible?

_____

_____

_____

_____

What Do I Need To Further Study From This Verse?

_____

_____

_____

_____

Bible Study

Date:

Today's Study

Scripture

Praise

Prayer

S.O.A.P.

Scripture

Observation

Application

Prayer

Reflection

What Is This Scripture Telling Me?

_____

_____

_____

_____

Why Did God Include This Scripture In The Bible?

_____

_____

_____

_____

What Do I Need To Further Study From This Verse?

_____

_____

_____

_____

Monday

Today's Goals

Tuesday

Today's Goals

Wednesday

Today's Goals

Thursday

Today's Goals

Friday

Today's Goals

Saturday

Today's Goals

Sunday

Today's Goals

Notes

Bible Study

Date:

Today's Study

Scripture

Praise

Prayer

S.O.A.P.

Scripture

Observation

Application

Prayer

Reflection

What Is This Scripture Telling Me?

_____

_____

_____

_____

Why Did God Include This Scripture In The Bible?

_____

_____

_____

_____

What Do I Need To Further Study From This Verse?

_____

_____

_____

_____

Bible Study

Date:

Today's Study

Scripture

Praise

Prayer

S.O.A.P.

Scripture	Observation

Application	Prayer

Reflection

What Is This Scripture Telling Me?

_____

_____

_____

_____

Why Did God Include This Scripture In The Bible?

_____

_____

_____

_____

What Do I Need To Further Study From This Verse?

_____

_____

_____

_____

Bible Study Date:

Today's Study

Scripture

Praise

Prayer

S.O.A.P.

Scripture

Observation

Application

Prayer

Reflection

What Is This Scripture Telling Me?

_____

_____

_____

_____

Why Did God Include This Scripture In The Bible?

_____

_____

_____

_____

What Do I Need To Further Study From This Verse?

_____

_____

_____

_____

Bible Study   Date:

Today's Study

Scripture

_____
_____
_____
_____
_____
_____
_____
_____
_____
_____
_____
_____
_____
_____
_____
_____

Praise

Prayer

S.O.A.P.

Scripture

Observation

Application

Prayer

Reflection

What Is This Scripture Telling Me?

_____

_____

_____

_____

_____

Why Did God Include This Scripture In The Bible?

_____

_____

_____

_____

What Do I Need To Further Study From This Verse?

_____

_____

_____

_____

Bible Study Date:

Today's Study

Scripture

_____

_____

_____

_____

_____

_____

_____

_____

_____

_____

_____

_____

_____

_____

_____

_____

_____

_____

_____

_____

Praise

Prayer

S.O.A.P.

Scripture

Observation

Application

Prayer

Reflection

What Is This Scripture Telling Me?

_____

_____

_____

_____

Why Did God Include This Scripture In The Bible?

_____

_____

_____

_____

What Do I Need To Further Study From This Verse?

_____

_____

_____

_____

Bible Study Date:

Today's Study

Scripture

Praise

Prayer

S.O.A.P.

Scripture	Observation

Application	Prayer

Reflection

What Is This Scripture Telling Me?

_____

_____

_____

_____

Why Did God Include This Scripture In The Bible?

_____

_____

_____

_____

What Do I Need To Further Study From This Verse?

_____

_____

_____

_____

Bible Study Date:

Today's Study

Scripture

Praise

Prayer

S.O.A.P.

Scripture	Observation

Application	Prayer

Reflection

What Is This Scripture Telling Me?

_____

_____

_____

_____

Why Did God Include This Scripture In The Bible?

_____

_____

_____

_____

What Do I Need To Further Study From This Verse?

_____

_____

_____

_____

Monday

Today's Goals

Tuesday

Today's Goals

Wednesday

Today's Goals

Thursday

Today's Goals

Friday

Today's Goals

Saturday

Today's Goals

Sunday

Today's Goals

Notes

Bible Study   Date:

Today's Study

Scripture

_____

_____

_____

_____

_____

_____

_____

_____

_____

_____

_____

_____

_____

_____

_____

_____

_____

_____

Praise

Prayer

S.O.A.P.

Scripture

Observation

Application

Prayer

Reflection

What Is This Scripture Telling Me?

_____

_____

_____

_____

Why Did God Include This Scripture In The Bible?

_____

_____

_____

_____

What Do I Need To Further Study From This Verse?

_____

_____

_____

_____

Bible Study Date:

Today's Study

Scripture

_____
_____
_____
_____
_____
_____
_____
_____
_____
_____

_____
_____
_____
_____
_____
_____
_____
_____
_____

Praise

Prayer

S.O.A.P.

Scripture

Observation

Application

Prayer

Reflection

What Is This Scripture Telling Me?

_____

_____

_____

_____

Why Did God Include This Scripture In The Bible?

_____

_____

_____

_____

What Do I Need To Further Study From This Verse?

_____

_____

_____

_____

Bible Study Date:

Today's Study

Scripture

Praise

Prayer

S.O.A.P.

Scripture

Observation

Application

Prayer

Reflection

What Is This Scripture Telling Me?

_____

_____

_____

_____

Why Did God Include This Scripture In The Bible?

_____

_____

_____

_____

What Do I Need To Further Study From This Verse?

_____

_____

_____

_____

Bible Study

Date:

Today's Study

Scripture

Praise

Prayer

S.O.A.P.

Scripture	Observation

Application	Prayer

Reflection

What Is This Scripture Telling Me?

_____

_____

_____

_____

Why Did God Include This Scripture In The Bible?

_____

_____

_____

_____

What Do I Need To Further Study From This Verse?

_____

_____

_____

_____

Bible Study   Date:

Today's Study

Scripture

Praise

Prayer

S.O.A.P.

Scripture	Observation

Application	Prayer

Reflection

What Is This Scripture Telling Me?

_____

_____

_____

_____

Why Did God Include This Scripture In The Bible?

_____

_____

_____

_____

What Do I Need To Further Study From This Verse?

_____

_____

_____

_____

Bible Study Date:

Today's Study

Scripture

Praise

Prayer

S.O.A.P.

Scripture

Observation

Application

Prayer

Reflection

What Is This Scripture Telling Me?

_____

_____

_____

_____

Why Did God Include This Scripture In The Bible?

_____

_____

_____

_____

What Do I Need To Further Study From This Verse?

_____

_____

_____

_____

Bible Study

Date:

Today's Study

Scripture

Praise

Prayer

S.O.A.P.

Scripture

Observation

Application

Prayer

Reflection

What Is This Scripture Telling Me?

_____

_____

_____

_____

Why Did God Include This Scripture In The Bible?

_____

_____

_____

_____

What Do I Need To Further Study From This Verse?

_____

_____

_____

_____

Made in the USA
Las Vegas, NV
04 January 2025

15749845R00066